Welcome to
THE ULTIMATE
BASEBALL
TRIVIA BOOK

CONTENTS PAGE

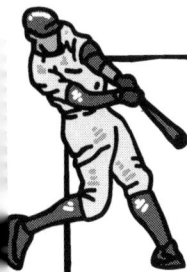

WARM-UP I

Some nice easy questions to get you warmed up!

1. In what city would you find the Marlins?

2. How many positions make up a baseball team?

3. What is a designated hitter?

4. What is the abbreviation ERA?

5. How many divisions are in each league (AL & NL)?

6. What are the minor leagues categorized as letters?

7. How many cities are home to 2 teams?

8. What is a home run with bases loaded called?

9. What are the 2 oldest MLB parks still in use today?

10. How many years did the Chicago Cubs go between winning World Series?

11. Whose nickname is "Mr. November" or "Captain Clutch"?

12. When do fans usually sing "Take Me Out to the Ball Game"?

13. What player is known for hitting the "Shot Heard 'Round the World"?

14. On average, how many balls are used during a typical baseball game: a) 25 b) 50 c) 100 or d) 150?

15. What base is stolen the most?

16. What is the most popular food to eat at a baseball game?

17. What state has generated the fewest professional baseball players?

18. Now the opposite. Which state as generated the most baseball players?

19. Who was nicknamed "Mr. Cub"?

20. "If you build it, he will come," is a quote from what movie?

WARM-UP II

Final warm-up round. Can you name all 30 MLB teams by division? Bonus points if you can put them in order of their 2021 regular season standings.

AL East	NL East

AL Central	NL Central

AL West	NL West

ROUND 1 - FOUNDING & HISTORY

1. In what year did the first recorded baseball game take place: a) 1749 b) 1809 c) 1897 or d) 1904

2. What was the name of the first professional baseball team, founded in the mid-1800's?

3. In 1919, the Giants and the Phillies played the shortest game in MLB history. How long did it last?

4. In what year was overhand pitching legalized?

5. What baseball rules, formalized in 1845, was based on the "New York Style" of play?

6. Who became the first MLB Commissioner?

7. What is "Beep Baseball" and who is it for?

8. What were the 2 original leagues?

9. Two other leagues developed, but only lasted one season. Can you name them?

10. When the American Association folded, 4 team still in existence today moved to the NL. Who were the teams?

11. Due to declining interest and attendance, how many of the 12 teams were cut after the 1900 season?

12. In 1899, what minor league seized the opportunity and declared itself a Major League team in 1904, creating the American League?

13. What document was signed that stated both the American and National Leagues were major leagues and the winner of each would play each other in the World Series to determine the overall winner?

14. In what year was said document signed?

15. What third Major League was announced in 1959?

16. Not surprising, it didn't last. Which of the two Major League did the above-mentioned league join?

17. In what city is the National Baseball Hall of Fame?

18. What year was the first MLB game aired on television?

19. Which two teams played in that game?

20. Exactly how many stitches must be on a baseball?

1. When did the Boston Red Sox win their first World Series?

2. Native Americans protested the 1995 World Series played by which two politically incorrect team names?

3. In the 1956 World Series between the Brooklyn Dodgers and New York Yankees, who threw a perfect Game 5?

4. What team won the very first World Series?

5. Who did that team defeat?

6. At 19 years and 180 days old, who was the youngest World Series player to hit a home run?

7. During the 1990s, how many seasons did the Braves make a World Series appearance?

8. Name the first pitcher to hit a grand slam during the World Series.

9. Letting the ball roll between his legs, who became the scapegoat for the Boston Red Sox losing the 1986 World Series?

10. Why didn't the 1904 World Series have a winner?

11. A typical World Series is a best-of-seven format. In 1903, 1919, 1920, and 1921, how many games were in the World Series in a "best-of" format?

12. What team has the record for most World Series titles?

13. What is the most common World Series match up: a) Yankees and Dodgers, b) Braves and Athletics, c) Red Sox and Reds, d) Cardinals and Tigers

14. What Astros player proposed to his girlfriend immediately after winning the 2017 World Series?

15. What stadium was the location of the first World Series game to be played in Texas?

16. Known as the "Show-Me-Series," what intrastate teams faced off in the 1985 World Series?

17. What was the first team to be swept in the World Series?

18. After being last place in the NL East by the 39th game of the season, what team turned their luck around to win the World Series?

19. What now division rivals faced off in what the media called the "Suds Series"?

20. Who holds the World Series record for most home runs with 18?

ROUND 3 - COACHES I

1. Who was the first to win Manager of the Year in both the American and National Leagues?

2. In 1907, the Boston Red Sox went through how many different managers?

3. What was the name of the Baltimore Orioles manager who was ejected from 91 games, setting a record?

4. Owner Philip K. Wrigley implemented the "College of Coaches" in 1961, meaning the Cubs would have a rotation of how many managers?

5. How many female coaches were there in the 2021 season?

6. Never having a losing record is quite the feat. What White Sox manager accomplished this?

7. What manager said, "I don't want to embarrass any other catchers by comparing him with Johnny Bench"?

8. Who brought the Indians their first World Series Championship in 1920?

9. Known for his unusually high batting stance, what former player became the Milwaukee Brewer's manager in 2015?

10. In 1965, the Mets hired what Olympian to be a running coach?

11. What manager of the Mets never actually managed a single game?

12. Who was the manager and owner of the Athletics, setting a record for the longest manager?

13. What movie starring Brad Pitt displayed a new player management theory by manager Billy Beane?

14. What manager won 2 World Series with the Pittsburgh Pirates?

15. What manager and former player had a head so large he had to have his helmet brought up from the minors, since the major leagues didn't have a helmet to fit his 8 1/8 hat size head?

16. Manager Branch Rickey was known for many things, like breaking the color line by signing Jackie Robinson from the Dodgers, inventing the farm system, and what offensive safety equipment?

17. Dennis Quaid played what pitching coach turned MLB player at age 35 in Disney's The Rookie?

18. Which manager was first to win 4 Manager of the Year Awards?

19. Who was the first female coach in MLB history?

20. Who became the first black female coach in professional baseball history?

ROUND 4 - FIRSTS

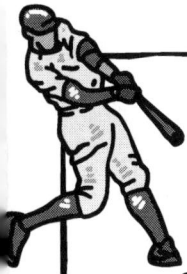

1. What team was the first to put numbers on the back of their jerseys?

2. What team played the very first MLB night game in 1935?

3. Who threw the first no-hitter in MLB history? What team was he on?

4. Who was the first player to hit for the cycle (single, double, triple, home run) in the MLB?

5. Who became the inaugural Rookie of the Year in 1947?

6. Who was the first African American to play in the Major League?

7. Who was the first team to win the World Series as a Wild Card team?

8. Who was the very first mascot and for what team?

9. Who was the first player to pitch a ball over 100mph?

10. What was the name of the first player to have his number retired?

11. Who was the first player to hit a home run, but never receive credit for it, because he was replaced by a pinch runner?

12. The cereal Wheaties is known for showcasing athletes. Who was the first baseball player to appear on the cereal box?

13. What 2-time Olympic softball gold medalist was the first woman to nationally call a televised playoff game?

14. Signed by the same team as Jackie Robinson, the Indianapolis Clowns, who was the first female to pitch in the Negro Leagues?

15. In 1894, who was the first player to hit four home runs in just one game?

16. Who was the first player to win the Gold Glove, MVP, Silver Slugger, and World Series in one season?

17. What player was the first to hit 50 double and 50 home runs in a single season?

18. In 1991, the Hall of Fame inducted its first Canadian player. What was his name?

19. What is the name of the first women to be inducted into the Hall of Fame?

20. What was the first team to use an airplane to travel in 1934?

Write the name of the first overall draft pick based on their team, position, and school they were drafted from.

Year	Pick Name	Pos - School
1982 (Cubs)		SS - Thomas Jefferson High
1983 (Twins)		RHP - Mount Vernon Nazarene
1984 (Mets)		OF - Mechanicsburg Area High
1985 (Brewers)		SS - North Carolina at Chapel Hill
1986 (Pirates)		SS - Arkansas
1987 (Mariners)		OF - Archbishop Mueller High
1988 (Padres)		RHP - Evansville
1989 (Orioles)		RHP - Louisiana State
1990 (Braves)		SS - The Bolles High
1991 (Yankees)		LHP - East Carteret High
1992 (Astros)		3B - California State at Fullerton
1993 (Mariners)		SS - Westminster Christian High
1994 (Mets)		RHP - Florida State
1995 (Angels)		OF - Nebraska
1996 (Pirates)		RHP - Clemson
1997 (Tigers)		RHP - Rice
1998 (Phillies)		3B - Miami
1999 (Rays)		OF - Athens Drive High
2000 (Marlins)		1B - Eastlake High
2001 (Twins)		C - Cretin High

Same again here with the last 20 picks!

Year	Pick Name	Pos - School
2002 (Pirates)		RHP - Ball State
2003 (Rays)		OF - Adolfo Camarillo High
2004 (Padres)		SS - Mission Bay High
2005 (D-Backs)		SS - Great Bridge High
2006 (Royals)		RHP - Tennessee
2007 (Rays)		LHP - Vanderbilt
2008 (Rays)		SS - Griffin High
2009 (Nationals)		RHP - San Diego State
2010 (Nationals)		OF - Southern Nevada College
2011 (Pirates)		RHP - UCLA
2012 (Astros)		SS - Puerto R. Baseball Academy
2013 (Astros)		RHP - Stanford
2014 (Astros)		LHP - Cathedral Catholic High
2015 (D-Backs)		SS - Vanderbilt
2016 (Phillies)		OF - La Costa Canyon High
2017 (Twins)		SS - JSerra Catholic High
2018 (Tigers)		RHP - Auburn
2019 (Orioles)		C - Oregon State
2020 (Tigers)		3B - Arizona State
2021 (Pirates)		C - Louisville

1. Youppi was the mascot for which Canadian team that no longer exists?

2. The Seattle Mariners had what type of antlered animal as their mascot?

3. What team's chicken mascot gave a rise in popularity to all other mascots?

4. Which team does not have a mascot, but used a "rally monkey" up until their 2002 World Series win?

5. Which team used a used white elephant during their early days in Philadelphia?

6. What team has 5 sausages that race at every home game?

7. What team has the Racing Presidents during the 7th inning stretch?

8. Which 3 teams do not have a mascot?

9. There are 6 mascots are in the Hall of Fame. Name 3.

10. Chief Noc-A-Homa was the mascot for which team, from 1966-1985?

11. In 1990, which team held a competition amongst its local elementary school students to design a new mascot?

12. Which teams mascot is called Blooper?

13. What is the name of the Cincinnati Reds' mascot?

14. What team's mascot is Wally the Green Monster?

15. What is the name of the Cleveland Indians' mascot?

16. What team's mascot is called Swinging Frair?

17. What kind of animal is Raymond the mascot?

18. What team's mascot is called Southpaw?

19. 'Weary Willie', the hobo clown, would often turn up to which teams games in the 1930s?

20. What team's mascot is called Lou Seal?

ROUND 8 - PITCHERS

1. What girl made history as the first female to pitch a shutout in the Little League World Series?

2. Who threw the last historic pitch in the Chicago Cubs 2016 World Series win?

3. Who set a league record of 59 consecutive innings without a run scored?

4. What pitcher clocked in at 6' 7" and 290 pounds?

5. A starter turned reliever recorded 84 consecutive saves, setting a league record?

6. What pitcher hit a 3-run homer off Madison Bumgerner in the 2016 National League Division Series Game 3?

7. Who was the first winner of the Cy Young award in both the American and National League?

8. What starting pitcher won the Cy Young award, yet had a losing record when he retired?

9. Diamondback pitcher Randy Johnson once hit what animal so hard with a pitch it exploded?

10. What left-handed pitcher holds the record for most career wins by a lefty?

11. By age 30, who became the youngest pitcher to reach the 300-game win mark?

12. What Hall of Fame pitcher had more walks than strikeouts?

13. Who threw the first perfect road game in MLB history?

14. What is the name of the oldest pitcher to register a win?

15. What Astros player was first in the league to be a perfect 15-0 at home in 2015?

16. Lefty Grove led the league in what stat more than any other pitcher?

17. Who was the first ever Cy Young Award winner?

18. What pitcher had more strikeouts than innings pitched?

19. What "disease" do pitchers get when they spontaneously lose the capability of throwing strikes?

20. Who started as a pitcher in front of a sold-out stadium just 20 days after his final high school baseball game?

ROUND 9 - DRAFTS

1. When was the first MLB draft?

2. Who was the number 1 overall draft pick from that year?

3. How many of the number 1 draft picks have gone on to be inducted into the Hall of Fame?

4. Although known for his stellar time with the Yankees, what shortstop did the Mariners draft in 1993?

5. Who drafted Tom Brady in 1995?

6. Who did the Arizona Diamond backs select first in the 1997 MLB Expansion Draft?

7. Who did the Tigers draft as their first ever pick?

8. Who was the first round draft pick to only played for the Colorado Rockies?

9. In what round was Ted Sizemore, National League Rookie of the Year, selected:
a) 1st, b) 4th, c) 11th, d) 15th

10. Who was the first infielder to be drafted first overall since Alex Rodriquez?

11. In the 1968 Expansion Draft, who did the Padres choose first?

12. What 6-time All-Star catcher from Florida State University was drafted 5th in the 2008 Draft?

13. Keith Hernandez was selected in which incredibly late round?

14. Who holds the record for the most high school home runs?

15. In 2004, the Oakland Athletics drafted what NFL quarterback in the 34th round?

16. Who was the 1999 number 1 draft pick who left for personal reason, then had an outstanding comeback in 2007?

17. What MLB team drafted the Kansas Chief QB Patrick Mahomes in 2014?

18. What high school in Tampa Bay, Florida has the most draft picks?

19. What year was the first time fans were allowed at the draft?

20. Ryne Sandberg was drafted by the Phillies in what round of the 1978 draft?

1. Does the MLB have a salary cap?

2. Who was the first highest-paid player in 1930 at $80,000?

3. How much was Hank Aaron's first professional contract with the Negro American League's Indianapolis Clowns: a) $200/month, b) $200/biweekly, c) $200/week, d) $200/game?

4. Who signed a contract for 10 years and $16 million, but it actually ended up being $23 million because of a "cost-of-living" clause?

5. Who was the first player to make $1 million in one season?

6. Who was the first player to earn $10 million in one season?

7. Who on the Philadelphia Phillies became the highest paid player in 1979?

8. What was the year and price on the contract that moved Babe Ruth from the Red Sox to the Yankees?

9. Who signed a contract that was voided after just one day by the Commissioner, leaving the athlete with a perfect on-base percentage?

10. Who did the Dodgers illegally sign, due to the player being under the age restriction?

11. Who must approve all contracts?

12. Whose contract didn't permit him to eat animal crackers in his bed?

13. Who signed a $330 million contract in 2019, then wore cleats with the team's new mascot on them for Opening Day?

14. Who signed the first $100 million contract in 1998?

15. Since then, how many $100 million + contracts were signed

16. In what year will the New York Mets complete their salary payments to Bobby Bonilla?

17. Whose contract included a $2 million incentive if he successfully made weight during six random weigh-ins during the season?

18. Who became a landlord for a Memphis apartment complex as part of his contract with the Kansas City Royals?

19. Houston Astros' owner Drayton McClane offered ace pitcher Roy Oswalt an addendum to his contract before Game 6 of the NLCS, stating Oswalt would receive what construction equipment if he won that game?

20. Charlie Kerfeld loved his number 37 so much, he received 37 boxes of what orange wiggly dessert as part of his contract?

ROUND 11 - POSTSEASON

1. When did the MLB start the first playoffs?

2. In what year did the MLB introduce the Wild Card?

3. In an 11-year span from 1995-2005, how many seasons did the Braves win the National League West division?

4. What year did the Astros finally win a game in November?

5. What Cardinals player was sidelined for the 1985 playoff, because the automatic tarp rolled over his leg while he was stretching?

6. What team started the season 1-8 in 2011 then made it to postseason with a record of 90-63?

7. Name the 4 players who played in the 1950s, 1960s and 1970s postseasons.

8. What team has the most consecutive postseason appearance?

9. What team won 100 regular season games and lost the 2004 World Series?

10. What pitcher has the record of most innings pitched in one postseason?

11. How many times has a player reached base because of catcher interference during the postseason, 13 times in the 2009 postseason alone?

12. How many players have hit postseason home runs on their birthday?

13. Who came back from a season-long injury to be the DH for the Chicago Cubs when they played in Cleveland in the World Series?

14. What central fielding position has had 22 different players hit home runs in the postseason?

15. Who saw the most pitches in the postseason with 2,749?

16. How many triple plays have been completed in postseason history: a) 0, b) 1, c) 2, or d) 4?

17. What year had the most walk off wins of any postseason series when the Minnesota Twins and Atlanta Braves met in the World Series?

18. In what season was an extra round of the playoff added because of the players strike?

19. What is the only team to have overcome a 3-0 deficit and gone on to win the World Series?

20. Causing a 10-day delay, what natural event happened in San Francisco during Game 3 of the 1989 World Series?

ROUND 12 - BABE RUTH

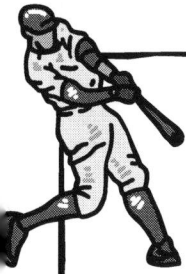

1. What 3 teams did Babe Ruth play for?
(Correctly identify at least 2)

2. What was the jinx called after Ruth left his first team?

3. What is his full name?

4. True or false, Babe was, and still is, the only player in the league to have the last name "Ruth"?

5. How did he get the nickname "Babe"?

6. His other nickname was "Sultan of _____."

7. How many home runs did Babe Ruth hit?

8. Who broke Ruth's home run record in 1974?

9. What position did Ruth start off playing?

10. What was unique about how he played that position?

11. What did Ruth claim as his birthday? Bonus: What is his birthday according to his birth certificate?

12. How many children did Babe have?

13. Why did Ruth spend time in jail?

14. Who was Babe's teammate who had a disease named after him?

15. How many World Series did the Red Sox win with Babe Ruth in 6 seasons?

16. How many World Series did the New York Yankees win with Babe Ruth in 15 seasons?

17. Who was the female pitcher to strike out Ruth in an exhibition game in 1931?

18. What candy bar, formerly named Kandy Kate, had its name changed allegedly for the baseball player?

19. After Ruth hit the first home run at the Yankee Stadium, what was the stadium nicknamed?

20. What batting record did Ruth break for 3 consecutive seasons in 1919, 1920, and 1921, breaking his own record in the latter two seasons?

ROUND 13 - JACKIE ROBINSON

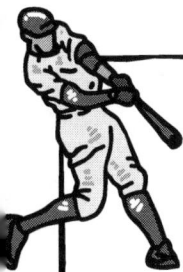

1. What was Jackie Robinson most known for?

2. On what team did Robinson make his MLB debut, becoming the first black player in an all-white league?

3. What movie was made about Robinson's life, with actor Chadwick Boseman portraying Robinson?

4. What other sport did Robinson play and earned a championship in while in high school?

5. During an All-Star game in high school, Robinson played with 2 future Hall of Famers, one from the Boston Red Sox and one from the Cleveland Indians. Who were they?

6. What President was the inspiration for Jackie's middle name, Roosevelt?

7. What day is now "Jackie Robinson Day" where all players were Number 42 for that day's game? What branch of military did Robinson serve in during WWII?

8. In what country did Robinson play Minor League Baseball? Can you name the team?

9. Close friends with Robinson, who was the first African American baseball player for the American League who made his debut the same season?

10. How many consecutive seasons was Robinson an All-Star?

11. What year did Robinson win the World Series with the Dodgers?

12. After retiring from baseball in 1956, Robinson went to work for what company?

13. Just a year after he began working there, Robinson became what executive-level position, making him the first African American of that position for any American company?

14. In what year did Robinson become the first African American inducted into the Baseball Hall of Fame?

15. A civil rights predominant figure himself, Robinson was called, "a legend and a symbol in his own time" by what well-known Civil Rights Movement leader?

16. What building became a National Historical Landmark in 1976 located in Brooklyn, New York?

17. Years after his retirement, Robinson broke another line, to become the first African American to hold a position as sports _____ on television.

18. What legislative branch award did Robinson posthumously receive in 2005?

19. What team(s) retired Robinson's number?

20. What day is now "Jackie Robinson Day" where all players were Number 42 for that day's game?

1. What type of illegal bat is assumed to be drilled out and filled with a lighter material?

2. A 1983 game between the New York Yankees and Kansas City Royals came to an abrupt end after the umpires deemed a bat used to hit the game winning home run had too tree sap, becoming known as what incident?

3. In 1947, what did the Cincinnati Redleg fans do to ensure their players made the starting lineup?

4. Who was the only umpire to be banned from baseball, because he worked with a gambler and was fixing the Detroit Wolverines games?

5. What league wide event unexpectedly ended the 1994 season, effectively ended the Expos chance to win the division?

6. In 1876, the Louisville Grays went from a sure fire conference win to suddenly blowing a significant standings lead, because players were getting paid to lose. How many players were banned for life because of this incident?

7. Name the Commissioner who banned Willie Mays and Mickey Mantle from baseball, because they were greeters at a casino, associating gambling with baseball?

8. What famous baseball player turned manager was found to be betting on games in 1989, and then received a lifetime ban?

9. What hard drug was commonplace in 1985 that lead to the Pittsburgh Drug Trials?

10. According to the 2007 Mitchell Report, 89 players allegedly had used performance enhancing drugs (steroids). Name three.

11. What year was the World Series between the Chicago White Sox and Cincinnati Reds rigged by the players and resulted in being called the Black Sox Scandal?

12. What infamous player, part of the Black Sox Scandal, was known for not wearing coverings on his feet after a particular pair hurt?

13. What type of substance did the small Florida clinic Biogenesis of America provide to clients such as Ryan Braun and Alex Rodriguez?

14. What instrument did the Houston Astros use to inform batting teammates about upcoming pitches in the 2017 season?

15. By the threat of the commissioner, what secret agreement occurred between team owners to restrict free agent contracts to pay lower salaries in the mid-80s for one of baseball's great scandals?

16. What is the name of the fan who, in 2003, reached over the wall at Wrigley Field to catch a foul ball, but instead deflected it away from outfielder Moises Alou, becoming the scapegoat for why the Cubs wouldn't make the World Series that year?

17. To prevent a scandal in 1908, an umpire refused a bribe from what team's doctor?

18. In a technological scandal, what team's scouting director hacked into the Houston Astros' database and stole information over the course of 2 years?

19. In 1972, Yankees players Mike Kekich and Fritz Peterson made an off-season trade of what?

20. What marketing ploy did the Cleveland Indians use to bring in fans that resulted in a ninth inning riot, forcing the game to be forfeited?

1. What does AAGPBL stand for?

2. How long was the AAGPBL active?

3. Why was the league created?

4. Who founded the league?

5. How many teams were in the league at its height?

6. What was the general geographical location of most the league's teams?

7. What was the league motto?

8. Which team won the first championship?

9. Which team won the most titles?

10. Did the women play in pants or skirts?

11. What did the players call the bruises they got from sliding?

12. How was the ball pitched: overhand or underhand?

13. What AAGPBL team had a movie made about them?

14. What was the movie title?

15. What famous actor played the coach and said, "There's no crying in baseball!"?

16. How much were the women paid a week: a) less than $45, b) $45-$85, c) $85-$105, d) more than $105?

17. Players had to be dressed up with their makeup and hair done anytime they were in public. True or false?

18. The "Rules of Conduct" mandated players couldn't smoke or drink publicly, must wear lipstick at all times, and had to keep their hair short or long?

19. In 1947, what Caribbean country hosted the spring training games?

20. How many AAGPBL players have been inducted into the National Women's Baseball Hall of Fame?

ROUND 16 - ALL-STAR GAME

1. When was the first All-Star Game?

2. In what city and stadium was the first All-Star Game played?

3. Does winning the All-Star game determine home field advantage in the upcoming World Series?

4. Who made the All-Star game as a second baseman and a catcher (not the same season)?

5. Who has the record for most All-Star Game appearances?

6. Who was the first player to hit a home run in an All-Star game in 1933?

7. After not being selected for the Diamondbacks' roster, but picked up by the Marlins with the Rule 5 draft, what player went on to make the All-Star game his rookie year of 2006?

8. Who was the first rookie to win a Home Run Derby?

9. What Giants player was in 20 All-Star Games?

10. What Tampa Bay Ray's pitcher got the 14th inning win in the 2008 All-Star Game?

11. In 2016, how many of the World Series Champion Chicago Cubs were voted into the All-Star game?

12. What pitcher started the 1980 All-Star Game, then only played one game after that due to a stroke?

13. What was shared last name of the two players who won the All-Star Game MVP, League MVP, and World Series MVP?

14. Who pitched 14 consecutive scoreless innings over multiple All-Star Games?

15. What city as hosted the most All-Star Games?

16. What is the name of the player to have been thrown out twice at home plate during a single All-Star game?

17. How many sets of brothers played in All-Star Games, either as teammates or opponents?

18. What U.S. President was a guest broadcaster for the 1989 All-Star game?

19. Only 1 player won back-to-back All-Star Game MVP. Who was it?

20. What Cardinals player is the league leader in All-Star Game home runs with 6?

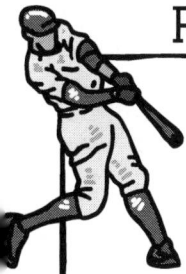

1. In what city are the College World Series played?

2. How many teams participate in the CWS?

3. What hard substance are bats made from at the collegiate level?

4. During his college career, who the first player to hit 100 home runs?

5. What school produced the most Number 1 draft picks?

6. What Southern University player has the NCAA Division I record for highest career batting average at .465?

7. What school won back-to-back championships in 2006 and 2007?

8. Because of those wins, what rival school reinstated their baseball program?

9. In collegiate baseball, a designated batter can also play what position on the field?

10. What is the name of the award given to the catcher of the year?

11. A mercy rule can apply when one team is ahead by how many runs after 7 innings?

12. In the MLB it's a best-of-seven series to win the World Series. How many games are in the Championship series for the CWS?

13. Who has the record for most consecutive game hitting streak at 58?

14. What school has won the College World Series Championship the most?

15. What late U.S. President was first baseman and captain of the 1948 Yale University Baseball Team?

16. What school has made the most CWS appearances with 36?

17. Who have been the last 3 CWS champions?

18. What school has appeared in the most CWS but never won a championship?

19. What conference has appeared the most in the CWS champions?

20. What is the name of the head coach who won 60 CWS games and 10 national championships, reaching the finals 5 consecutive years?

Round 18 - Hank Aaron

1. Hank is a nickname. What is Aaron's legal first name?

2. What are Aaron's baseball nicknames?

3. In what year did Aaron break the home run record previously held by Babe Ruth?

4. What other predominant outfield could Aaron have played with on the San Francisco Giants if they had offered Aaron $50 more a month?

5. How many seasons did Hank play with his younger brother on the Braves?

6. Aaron played for 2 different teams in 2 different cities but moved 3 times during his MLB career. Can you name the 3 relocations with the correct city and team?

7. How long was his MLB career?

8. How many records does Aaron still hold today? Bonus if you can name them all.

9. What is Aaron's RBI record that has yet to be broken?

10. What year was Aaron inducted into the Hall of Fame?

11. What was Aaron's autobiography titled, released in 1999?

12. Hank Aaron was idolized by many, including which famous African American boxer?

13. His highest paid salary for a single season was $240,000 by the Brewers. True or False?

14. How many Gold Glove Awards did Aaron earn?

15. What stadium has a bronze statue of Aaron to commemorate his historic career?

16. What award was presented to Hank Aaron in 2002?

17. What organization did Hank and his wife Billye found to assist underprivileged youth with scholarship opportunities?

18. Aaron won what hitting recognition back-to-back in 1955 and 1956?

19. Who broke their ankle during a spring training game to give Aaron a chance to start the season in the major leagues?

20. What manual job as a kid does Aaron credit his powerful wrists to help him turn on a pitch and hit the ball so well?

1. How many MLB teams have called a Canadian city home?

2. What player with a "tornadic" windup and delivery has been credited for opening the opportunity for Japanese players in the MLB?

3. In what country did Dal Maxvil hit the first major league international grand slam?

4. What country has the most Olympic baseball wins, never finishing with less than Bronze?

5. What country outside the U.S. has produced the most MLB players?

6. Per capita, what country generates the most major league players?

7. On 2021 Opening Day, how many different countries or territories did players originate from?

8. What city has hosted the most international Opening Day games?

9. What is a typical linguistic clause addition for international players to have in their contracts?

10. How many countries is baseball played in:
a) under 50, b) 50 – 75, c) 75 – 100, or d) over 100?

11. What country has the largest professional baseball league outside the United States?

12. In what European country is it assumed baseball actually originated in?

13. What game, similar to baseball is best known for being played in India?

14. When did baseball make its Olympic debut?

15. In what year did South Korea's KBO League have their first game?

16. Who was the first Japanese position player to play in the MLB?

17. The player from question 16 bats in a unique way. What is his batting style called?

18. The Australian Baseball League happens during an unusual time. What months do they play?

19. How many Cuban-born players appeared in the 2019 MLB season?

20. Besides the Olympics, what is the other international championship played, started in 2006?

ROUND 20 - NFL MVP

List the player who won the MVP in the last 10 years based on team and position for each league.

AL MVP

Year	Name	Team	Position
2011		Detroit Tigers	SP
2012		Detroit Tigers	3B
2013		Detroit Tigers	3B
2014		LA Angles	CF
2015		Toronto Blue Jays	3B
2016		LA Angles	CF
2017		Houston Astros	2B
2018		Boston Red Sox	OF
2019		LA Angles	CF
2020		Chicago White Sox	1B

NL MVP

Year	Name	Team	Position
2011		Milwaukee Brewers	OF
2012		San Francisco Giants	C
2013		Pittsburg Pirates	OF
2014		LA Dodgers	SP
2015		Washington Nationals	RF
2016		Chicago Cubs	3B
2017		Miami Marlins	RF
2018		Milwaukee Brewers	OF
2019		LA Dodgers	RF
2020		Atlanta Braves	1B

1. How many sets of brothers have played in the major leagues: a) 91, b) 162, c) 288, or d) 432?

2. Over 100 sets of brothers been teammates, true or false?

3. How many sets of twins have played in the MLB?

4. Who holds the record for the most home runs hit between brothers?

5. Who are considered the "Flying Molina's"?

6. Who were the first African American brothers to play on the same team in the Major League?

7. Who were the first father-son duo to play on a team together, hitting back-to-back home runs?

8. In 1998, two sets of brothers all played for the Cincinnati Reds in the same game, covering 1st, 2nd, and 3rd base and shortstop. What were the last names of both sets of brothers?

9. Who was the first pitcher to strike out his younger brother during the pitcher's MLB debut?

10. What two MVP players from the 1960s and 1970s shared the same last name but were not related?

11. What three brothers made up the outfield for the San Francisco Giants in 1963?

12. Felipe Alou had 2 sons, one a manager and the other a player. Which of his sons played outfield for the Cubs in 2003?

13. Joe DiMaggio is the most famous of his family, but 2 of his brothers also played professional baseball. What were their names?

14. What father-son duo with a last name most applicable to baseball both played for the Detroit Tigers during their careers?

15. In 1986 with a 5-year age gap, these two pitching brothers started their careers together, combining for 18 Gold Glove Awards. Who were they?

16. What brothers were nicknamed "Big Poison" and "Little Poison"?

17. What father-son duo recorded over 1,000 home runs between the two of them?

18. A "battery" is a pitcher-catcher duo. Who were the first brother battery?

19. What manager, who led the 1988 Dodgers to a World Series win, had two sons named Jose and Andy play in the MLB?

20. How many generations of Boone's have played in the major leagues?

1. Can you list all the original American League teams (some may not be the names we know today)?

2. Who won the Triple Crown (batting average, home runs, and RBIs) in 1933?

3. When did the last AL team join the league?

4. Setting an American League record, what pitcher won at least 11 games a season for 17 consecutive seasons?

5. What team was their first AL Championship in 1901, the team's inaugural season?

6. What pitcher has the AL record for most wins in a season at 41 wins?

7. Who set the AL record for most consecutive games at 2nd base without an error at 104 games?

8. Who won the AL batting championship without hitting a home run during the whole season?

9. Which AL team has the most Cy Young Award winners at 7?

10. What team has had more back-to-back World Series than any other team in the MLB?

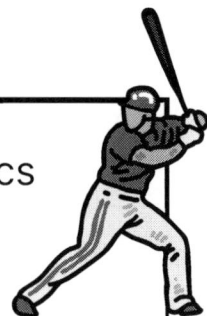

11. With 16, the Philadelphia/Kansas City/Oakland Athletics hold the record for the most 100+ game _____?

12. In 91 All-Star Games, the American League has won how many times?

13. What is the most recent AL team to change their name? What did they change it to?

14. The first Hall of Fame induction ceremony in 1936 had 3 of the 5 players hailing from the American League. It was the New York Yankees, Washington Senators and what other team?

15. Who was the first team in the MLB to reach 100 game winning season, and did it 2 seasons in a row?

16. What player is credited for setting the most MLB records (90), including highest career batting average at .367 and career batting titles with 11 (some sources say 12) and played his entire career for two AL teams?

17. Who is the only player to have won the AL batting title, AL MVP, and AL Rookie of the year in a single season?

18. What major city did the original Milwaukee Brewers team relocate to in 1901?

19. What team was the last to be enfranchised in the AL?

20. Which cities have continuously hosted four of the original eight teams since the inception of the league?

1. Can you list all the original National League teams after the reduction of teams in 1900 (some might not be known by the same names as they are today)?

2. When was the National League formed?

3. In 1930, who batted .303?

4. What team has won the most titles of all the NL teams?

5. When did the San Francisco Giants win their first NL Championship?

6. Why was St. Louis expelled from the National League in 1877?

7. Who is the youngest player to have won the NL MVP at what age?

8. Which is the most recent team to join the NL?

9. Which is the oldest NL team to never have an MVP?

10. In the first 100 seasons of the league, what team has won the most games?

11. The Cubs, Giants, and what other NL team won back-to-back World Series?

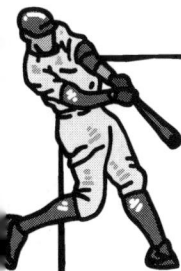

12. In an unlucky statistic, what NL team had the most 100+ game losing seasons?

13. Which team had the most Cy Young Award winners with 12?

14. What NL team has the most MVP winners with 17, coming in second overall?

15. What NL team has changed their name the most, which makes sense, since they're the oldest team in the major leagues?

16. Which team is the oldest to have originated in the city they're still in?

17. What team only lasted a single season in 1880, because they wouldn't stop selling beer?

18. What modern-day team had team names like "Bridegroom," "Grays," "Robins," and "Superbas"?

19. What was the lowest fan attendance count at a 2011 game between the Cincinnati Reds and Florida Marlins?

20. The National League had the first ever game announced over what type of broadcast, which was between the Philadelphia Phillies and Pittsburgh Pirates?

ROUND 24 - OPENING DAY

1. Who were the teams to play on the very first Opening Day?

2. Which U.S. President was the first Commander in Chief to throw out a ceremonial first pitch on Opening Day?

3. Who are the only 3 U.S. presidents to not throw out the ceremonial first pitch on Opening Day?

4. Who was the Opening Day starting pitcher for the White Sox from 2002-2006 and 2008-2011?

5. Which two westward expansion teams met on Opening Day in 1958?

6. In what country did the Colorado Rockies play on Opening Day 1999?

7. On Opening Day 2006, the Marlins had how many rookies starting?

8. Who did the Padres beat in their inaugural game?

9. Who was the first pitcher to hit 2 home runs on Opening Day?

10. What Seattle based rapper sang his song "My Oh My" in memory of play-by-play announcer Dave Niehaus on Opening Day 2011?

11. What rookie Toronto Blue Jay's player hit a home run during his first at-bat in the Jay's inaugural game, 1997?

12. In 1940, who was the only player to throw an Opening Day no-hitter?

13. What pitcher has the most Opening Day starts with 16?

14. What team has the best winning percentage on Opening Day?

15. In what year did the Opening Day riot of New York force the first game to be cancelled?

16. What southside team's fans went streaking on Opening Day 1974?

17. How many innings was the longest Opening Day game in history?

18. How many Opening Days were delayed due to lockouts or strikes?

19. What catcher said, "A home opener is always exciting, no matter if it's home or on the road"?

20. What player, nicknamed "Big Donkey", has 8 career Opening Day home runs, tied with Hall of Famers Frank Robinson and Ken Griffey Jr?

How well do you know your AL stadium names?
Write the correct team on each row.

Team	Stadium	Capacity	Built
	Angel Stadium	45,517	1966
	Comerica Park	41,083	2000
	Fenway Park	37,755	1912
	Globe Life Field	40,300	1989
	Guaranteed Rate Field	40,615	1991
	Kauffman Stadium	37,903	1973
	Minute Maid Park	41,168	2000
	Orioles Park at Camden Yards	45,971	1992
	Progressive Field	34,788	1994
	RingCentral Coliseum	46,847	1966
	Rogers Centre	49,282	1989
	T-Mobile Park	47,929	1999
	Target Field	38,544	2010
	Tropicana Field	25,000	1990
	Yankee Stadium	47,309	2009

Same again here but with NL teams!

Team	Stadium	Capacity	Built
	Busch Stadium	45,494	2006
	Chase Field	48,686	1998
	Citi Field	41,922	2009
	Citizens Bank Park	42,792	2004
	Coors Field	50,445	1995
	Dodger Stadium	56,000	1962
	Great American Ball Park	42,319	2003
	Marlins Park	36,742	2012
	Miller Park	41,900	2001
	Nationals Park	41,339	2008
	Oracle Park	14,915	2000
	Petco Park	40,209	2004
	PNC Park	38,747	2001
	SunTrust Park	41,084	2017
	Wrigley Field	41,649	1914

Round 27 - Famous Jerseys

Can you match these players with their iconic jersey numbers? Draw a line to connect the name to the number.

Pete Rose	66
CC Sabathia	2
Barry Bonds	30
Joe DeMaggio	24
David Ortiz	3
Alex Rodriguez	38
Jackie Robinson	13
Willie Mays	34
Randy Johnson	5
Babe Ruth	99
Rickey Henderson	44
Roberto Clemente	35
Derek Jeter	21
Aaron Judge	51
Lou Gehrig	23
Nolan Ryan	42
Curt Shilling	4
Ryne Sandberg	52
Yasiel Puig	25
Hank Aaron	14

ARIZONA DIAMONDBACKS

1. In what year did the Diamondbacks play their inaugural game?

2. How many Diamondback players made appearances in a 19-inning game against the St. Louis Cardinals in 2019:
a) 18 b) 24) c) 30 d) 37

3. What player appeared in an episode of The Simpson titled "Bart has Two Mommies"?

4. Who was the manager for the 2001 World Series win?

5. With 3 2-run homers and a 3-run double, what player had 9 RBIs in one game?

ATLANTA BRAVES

1. The Braves have called 3 cities home: Boston, Milwaukee, and now Atlanta. Who is the only player to have played in all 3 locations?

2. In 2005, the Braves had how many rookies on their roster: a) 6, b) 9, c) 12, d) 18

3. Name the pitcher who hit 2 grand slams in a single game.

4. How many losing seasons did the Braves have their 13 years in Milwaukee?

5. Chipper is his nickname. What is Jones' legal name?

BALTIMORE ORIOLES

1. During their time as the St. Louis Browns, outfielder Pete Gray played a special way. What made him unique?

2. Nicknamed "The Iron Man," who played the most consecutive games?

3. In a poor season performance in 2018, how many games did the team lose?

4. Only one player has ever hit a home run out of the Memorial Stadium. Who was it?

5. The Orioles defeated what team to clinch their first World Series?

BOSTON RED SOX

1. What is the "Curse of the Bambino"?

2. With a .344 career batting average, who set the franchise record?

3. Who did the Red Sox play and beat in the 1916 World Series?

4. Who stole 70 bases during one season?

5. What MVP winner had to retire due to his immense fear of flying and panic attacks in the airport?

CHICAGO CUBS

1. What animal is the curse symbol for why the Cubs hadn't won a World Series in 108 years?

2. In the off-season, Fergie Jenkins played for a family-fun entertainment basketball organization. What is the organization called?

3. Although traded now, who earned the nickname El Mago as the Cubs' middle infielder and what does it mean?

4. What legendary Cub's announcer also has a restaurant named after him in Wrigleyville?

5. What player was nicknamed "Mr. Sunshine"?

CHICAGO WHITE SOX

1. In 1994, what legendary Chicago Bulls player tried out for the White Sox?

2. Who was nicknamed "The Big Hurt"?

3. The White Sox traded Mike Cameron in 1998, and who did they receive in return?

4. Where did the team originate from and what were they called?

5. Who earned the most strikeouts in a single season franchise record?

CINCINNATI REDS

1. What nickname did the Reds use in the 1970s?

2. Joe Nuxhall was the youngest player to have played in the MLB. How old was he when he made his debut?

3. How many games long was Pete Rose' hitting streak?

4. How many official mascots do the Reds have? Bonus if you can name them all.

5. In 1968, what rookie catcher won the Gold Glove Award?

CLEVELAND INDIANS

1. What Cleveland's original baseball name?

2. What was the Cleveland Municipal Stadium nickname, based off its scorching summer nights, frigid lake air, and swarms of bugs?

3. What was the team's longest game win streak?

4. What movie starring Charlie Sheen was based on the Cleveland Indians?

5. How many consecutive games were sold out at Jacobs Field, prompting the team to retire that number in honor its the fans?

COLORADO ROCKIES

1. There is a string of purple seats at the Coors Field all the way around the stadium's third level. Why are they purple?

2. In 2007, what league single-season record did the team break?

3. How many bricks built the Coors Field: a) 847,000 b) 1.4 million, c) 3.6 million, d) 8.1 million

4. Who was the first player to have over 40 saves in a single season?

5. When did the Rockies appear in their first World Series?

DETROIT TIGERS

1. Pitcher Joel Zumaya missed 3 games, because he hurt himself playing what Xbox musical video game?

2. What 10-time Gold Glove right fielder was known as "Mr. Tiger"?

3. In 1934, the Tigers were known by what nickname?

4. What obscure dining room item did Norm Cash bring up to bat?

5. In 1971, who became the first player to have a heart attack and return as an active player a year later?

HOUSTON ASTROS

1. What was Houston's original team name?

2. What was special about the Atros' colorful uniforms they unveiled in 1975?

3. Who were the "Killer B's"?

4. Who was the pitcher who got hit in the face while at bat and had his left orbital bone broken?

5. What player married Kate Upton just days after the World Series in 2017?

KANSAS CITY ROYALS

1. What livestock show and rodeo was the team named after?

2. The Royals lost a franchise record-setting how many games in 2005?

3. In 1975, who replaced manager Jack McKeon, paving the way for the Royals to become a dominant team?

4. What batter had the most strikeouts in a single season?

5. Whose batting average around .400 all season was the franchise highest single season batting average?

LOS ANGELES ANGELS

1. What is the name of the team's Rally Monkey?

2. The youngest player to ever reach 100 home runs and 100 stolen bases was who?

3. Who was the pitcher born without a right hand?

4. What singing cowboy originally owned the Angels?

5. Who was nicknamed "Nureyev"?

LOS ANGELES DODGERS

1. Who was the broadcaster who called 67 years of Dodger baseball?

2. Who was the pitcher who led the MLB in ERA for 4 consecutive seasons?

3. The name "Dodgers" referred to dodging what?

4. In 1974, the Dodgers broke the glass ceiling by allowing what female journalist into the locker room?

5. Who wore number 99 for both the Red Sox and Dodgers?

MIAMI MARLINS

1. In 2019, how many starting pitchers had winning records by the end of the season?

2. Who hit a grand slam during his debut at-bat with the Marlins?

3. Who did the Marlins sign as their first player?

4. Name the Marlins' first manager in 1992.

5. In what year did the Florida Marlins move from Miami Gardens to downtown, becoming the Miami Marlins?

MILWAUKEE BREWERS

1. What was the Brewers original location and team name?

2. What is the longest game in franchise history:
a) 5 hours 42 minutes, b) 6 hours 57 minutes, c) 8 hours 6 minutes, or d) 9 hours 12 minutes?

3. What Brewers broadcaster starred in Mr. Belvedere from 1985-1990?

4. Whose number was retired by the Brewers and the Athletics?

5. What player holds the Brewers record for at-bats, doubles, triples, hits, total bases, and strikeouts, playing his entire career with Milwaukee?

MINNESOTA TWINS

1. What are the Minnesota Twins named after?

2. Who played each of the 9 positions in a one game, rightfully nicknamed "Mr. Versatility"?

3. Cotton Nash played for which two NBA teams during the 1964-65 season?

4. When was the team relocated to Minnesota?

5. In what year did the Twins set a new record, becoming the first team to hit 300 home runs?

NEW YORK METS

1. Johan Santana was the first pitcher to throw a no-hitter in the franchise's history. What year did that occur?

2. What former college standout quarterback signed a minor league contract with the Mets?

3. What is "Met" short for?

4. Famous people love to play for the Mets. What country music star was invited to partake in 2000 Spring Training?

5. Who did the Mets trade in "the Midnight Massacre," leaving the team to wallow in last place for the years following?

NEW YORK YANKEES

1. Who is the only player to earn Rookie of the Year and MVP?

2. Who leads the team in all-time career hits?

3. With the nickname "Godzilla," who made a cameo in Godzilla Against Mechagodzilla?

4. What was the 1927 batting lineup called?

5. What was the team's original name?

OAKLAND ATHLETICS

1. How few games did the A's win in the 1916 season, which was the lowest since 1900?

2. Who is "Mr. October"?

3. How many bases did Mark McGwire attend to steal in his career? How many times was he successful?

4. In their first 7 seasons, how many times did they have a winning season?

5. Named after an animal with long whiskers, who was the first Athletics player to get his number retired?

PHILADELPHIA PHILLIES

1. Who set the record for most bases stolen in a season without getting caught?

2. The Philies lost how many games in a row in 1961: a) 0, b) 23, c) 31, or d) 44

3. According to a fan vote, what were the Phillis called for the 1944 season?

4. What year was "The Greatest Collapse in Baseball History"?

5. In just one season, who stole 111 bases?

PITTSBURG PIRATES

1. The Pirates adopted what famous Sister Sledge song in 1979 as their theme song?

2. Honus Wagner earned a nickname at shortstop based off his German heritage and speed, same as a curse ghost pirate ship. What was his nickname?

3. What pitcher tragically died in a plane crash on his way to deliver aid after an earthquake in Nicaragua?

4. What 2017 infielder had awful luck, getting hit by a pitch in 4 consecutive at-bats?

5. What was the reason for the team changing its name to the Pirates?

SAN DIEGO PADRES

1. During a doubleheader, who hit 5 home runs in one day?

2. What fast food chain owner and new team owner said, "Ladies and gentlemen, I suffer with you"?

3. In 1969, upon joining the MLB, in how many consecutive seasons did the Padres come in last place?

4. "Mr. Padre" won 8 league batting titles. What was his real name?

5. Who was the Padres first owner, convicted of embezzling nearly $9 million?

SAN FRANCISCO GIANTS

1. When did the Giants play in their first World Series appearance?

2. What Giants player broke Hank Aaron's home run record?

3. In Game 1 of the 2014 World Series, who had a .29 ERA?

4. How many consecutive innings from June 1979 to May 1982 did Greg Minton not allow a home run?

5. For 18 consecutive seasons, who lead the team in home runs?

SEATTLE MARINERS

1. After their foundation in 1977, how long did it take for the Mariners to have a winning season?

2. The Mariners set a league record for using how many pitchers to combine for a no-hitter against the Dodgers in 2012?

3. What third baseman tried to blow a slow rolling ball foul, stating there was a "no-blow rule"?

4. How many teams were involved in a 12-player trade that led Franklin Gutierrez to the Mariners?

5. In 2019, the Mariners recorded the most pitchers used during a single season. How many pitchers did they use?

ST LOUIS CARDINALS

1. Who bought the team in 1953 to keep the Cardinals in St. Louis and has the current stadium named after him?

2. What is the name of the only player to bat .400 and have 40 home runs in a single season?

3. What baserunner ignored the third base coach's signs in the 1946 World Series, making "Slaughter's Mad Dash" to score the game-winning run in Game 7?

4. Who hit 3 home runs in Game 3 of the 2011 World Series, joining Babe Ruth and Reggie Jackson as the only other players to achieve this?

5. In 1995, Anheuser-Busch Brewery sold the Cardinals to the Williams DeWitt Jrs's investment group, for how much money: a) $87 million, b) $114 million, c) 138 million, or d) $147 million?

TAMPA BAY RAYS

1. What was the team's name prior to being purchased by Stuart Sternberg in 2007? Devil Rays

2. What horror genre novelist was the scapegoat for the Ray's 2002 15-game losing streak?

3. Who lead the league in saves in 2017?

4. In 2016, what outfield broke 2 bones in his left hand extending out for a line drive?

5. What pitcher threw the ball that broke Sammy Sosa's bat, exposing the cork?

TEXAS RANGERS

1. What general manager left the team after just 18 hours with a 1-0 record?

2. Who is "The Human Rain Delay," nicknamed for his extensive batting routine?

3. Kenny Rogers' 1994 perfect game was saved by a catch from what player?

4. What player won the most Gold Glove Awards (13) of any catcher in MLB history?

5. Who was known for "doctoring baseballs" (i.e. throwing spitballs)?

TORONTO BLUE JAYS

1. What organization was the original owner of the Blue Jays?

2. Pitcher Dave Stieb had a brutal curveball that became known as what?

3. Whose nickname was "Doc"?

4. What was the name of the first mascot?

5. What player stole second base, third base, and home plate in a single inning?

WASHINGTON NATIONALS

1. Before 2005, where was the team located and what were they called?

2. How many runs did the team earn in its highest scoring game: a) 11, b) 18, c) 22, or d) 25?

3. In 2009, the team had a misspelling on their jerseys. How was the name misspelled?

4. What pitcher completed a full game, giving up 0 earned runs and still lost?

5. How many players did the Nationals trade to acquire Gio Gonzalez? Bonus if you know who they were?

ANSWERS

Warm Up I

1. Miami
2. Nine
3. An assigned batter to take the place of a pitcher in the batting lineup
4. Earned Run Average
5. 3 divisions in each league, 6 total
6. AAA (Triple A), AA (Double A), A (Single A), all acceptable answers
7. 3 cities
8. Grand slam
9. Fenway Park and Wrigley Field
10. 108 Years
11. Derek Jeter
12. 7th inning stretch
13. Bobby Thomson
14. C) 100 baseballs
15. 2nd base
16. Hot dogs
17. Alaska
18. California
19. Ernie Banks
20. Field of Dreams

Warm Up II

AL East	NL East
Tampa Bay Rays	Atlanta Braves
New York Yankees	Philadelphia Phillies
Boston Red Sox	New York Mets
Toronto Blue Jays	Miami Marlins
Baltimore Orioles	Washington Nationals
AL Central	**NL Central**
Chicago White Sox	Milwaukee Brewers
Cleveland Indians	St. Louis Cardinals
Detroit Tigers	Cincinnati Reds
Kansas City Royals	Chicago Cubs
Minnesota Twins	Pittsburg Pirates
AL West	**NL West**
Houston Astros	San Francisco Giants
Seattle Mariners	Los Angeles Dodgers
Oakland Athletics	San Diego Padres
Los Angeles Angels	Colorado Rockies
Texas Rangers	Arizona Diamondbacks

Round 1 - Founding & History
1. A) 1749
2. Cincinnati Red Stockings
3. 51 minutes
4. 1884
5. Knickerbocker Rules
6. Kenesaw Mountain Landis in 1912
7. A type of baseball for the blind
8. National League and American Association
9. Union Association and Players League
10. Cardinals, Dodgers, Pirates, and Reds
11. 4 teams
12. Western League
13. National Agreement
14. 1903
15. Continental League
16. National League
17. Cooperstown, New York
18. 1936
19. Brooklyn Dodgers and Cincinnati Reds
20. 108

Round 2 - Super Bowl History
1. 1903
2. Atlanta Braves and Cleveland Indians
3. Don Larsen
4. Boston Americans
5. Pittsburgh Pirates
6. Andruw Jones
7. 5 times
8. Dave McNally

9. Bill Buckner
10. New York Giants refused to play the Boston Red Sox because of business rivalries between leagues.
11. 9 games
12. New York Yankees
13. A) Yankees and Dodgers
14. Jose Altuve
15. Minute Maid Park
16. Kansas City Royals and St. Louis Cardinals
17. Houston Astros by the Chicago White Sox
18. Miami Marlins
19. Milwaukee Brewers and St. Louis Cardinals
20. Mickey Mantle

Round 3 - Coaches I
1. Bobby Cox
2. 5 managers
3. Earl Weaver
4. 9 managers
5. 23 female coaches
6. Al Lopez
7. Sparky Anderson
8. Tris Speaker
9. Craig Counsell
10. Jesse Owens
11. Carlos Beltran
12. Connie Mack
13. Moneyball
14. Danny Murtaugh
15. Bruce Bochy
16. Batting helmet
17. Joe/Jimmy Morris
18. Tony LaRussa
19. Justine Siegal
20. Bianca Smith

Round 4 - Firsts

1. Yankees
2. Cincinnati Reds
3. George Bradley for the Cardinals
4. Curry Foley
5. Jackie Robinson
6. Moses Fleetwood Walker in 1884
7. Florida Marlins (before they became the Miami Marlins)
8. Mr. Met for the New York Mets in 1964
9. Nolan Ryan
10. Lou Gehrig
11. Bengie Molina. It was ruled a single, therefore he was replaced by pinch runner Emmanuel Burriss. Through instant replay, the umps determined it was a home run, so Burriss crossed home plate and received the credit (one of the more obscure ones I found, so if people have questions, you have an answer!)
12. Robin Yount
13. Jessica Mendoza
14. Mamie "Peanut" Johnson
15. Bobby Lowe
16. Mookie Betts
17. Albert Belle
18. Ferguson "Fergie" Jenkins
19. Effa Louise Manley
20. Cincinnati Reds

Round 5 - First Round Draft Picks I

Year	Pick Name	Pos - School
1982 (Cubs)	Shawon Dunston	SS - Thomas Jefferson High
1983 (Twins)	Tim Belcher	RHP - Mount Vernon Nazarene
1984 (Mets)	Shawn Abner	OF - Mechanicsburg Area High
1985 (Brewers)	B.J. Surhoff	SS - North Carolina at Chapel Hill
1986 (Pirates)	Jeff King	SS - Arkansas
1987 (Mariners)	Ken Griffey Jr.	OF - Archbishop Mueller High
1988 (Padres)	Andy Benes	RHP - Evansville
1989 (Orioles)	Ben McDonald	RHP - Louisiana State
1990 (Braves)	Chipper Jones	SS - The Bolles High
1991 (Yankees)	Brien Taylor	LHP - East Carteret High
1992 (Astros)	Phil Nevin	3B - California State at Fullerton
1993 (Mariners)	Alex Rodriguez	SS - Westminster Christian High
1994 (Mets)	Paul Wilson	RHP - Florida State
1995 (Angels)	Darin Erstad	OF - Nebraska
1996 (Pirates)	Kris Benson	RHP - Clemson
1997 (Tigers)	Matt Anderson	RHP - Rice
1998 (Phillies)	Pat Burrell	3B - Miami
1999 (Rays)	Josh Hamilton	OF - Athens Drive High
2000 (Marlins)	Adrian Gonzalez	1B - Eastlake High
2001 (Twins)	Joe Mauer	C - Cretin High

Round 6 - First Round Draft Picks II

Year	Pick Name	Pos - School
2002 (Pirates)	Bryan Bullington	RHP - Ball State
2003 (Rays)	Delmon Young	OF - Adolfo Camarillo High
2004 (Padres)	Matt Bush	SS - Mission Bay High
2005 (D-Backs)	Justin Upton	SS - Great Bridge High
2006 (Royals)	Luke Hochevar	RHP - Tennessee
2007 (Rays)	David Price	LHP - Vanderbilt
2008 (Rays)	Tim Beckham	SS - Griffin High
2009 (Nationals)	Stephen Strasburg	RHP - San Diego State
2010 (Nationals)	Bryce Harper	OF - Southern Nevada College
2011 (Pirates)	Gerrit Cole	RHP - UCLA
2012 (Astros)	Carlos Correa	SS - Puerto R. Baseball Academy
2013 (Astros)	Mark Appel	RHP - Stanford
2014 (Astros)	Brady Aiken	LHP - Cathedral Catholic High
2015 (D-Backs)	Dansby Swanson	SS - Vanderbilt
2016 (Phillies)	Mickey Moniak	OF - La Costa Canyon High
2017 (Twins)	Royce Lewis	SS - JSerra Catholic High
2018 (Tigers)	Casey Mize	RHP - Auburn
2019 (Orioles)	Adley Rutschman	C - Oregon State
2020 (Tigers)	Spencer Torkelson	3B - Arizona State
2021 (Pirates)	Henry Davis	C - Louisville

Round 7 - Mascots

1. Montreal Expos
2. Moose
3. San Diego
4. Anaheim/Los Angeles Angels
5. Oakland Athletics
6. Milwaukee Brewers
7. Washington Nationals
8. Los Angeles Angels, Los Angeles Dodgers, New York Yankees
9. Mr. Met, Oriole Bird, Phillie Phanatic, Slider, Sluggerrr, and San Diego Chicken
10. Atlanta Braves
11. Houston Astros
12. Atlanta Braves
13. Mr Red
14. Boston Red Sox
15. Slider
16. San Diego Padres
17. Cownose stingray, accept stingray
18. Chicago White Sox
19. Brooklyn Dodgers
20. San Francisco Giants

Round 8 - Quarterbacks

1. Mo'ne Davis
2. Mike Montgomery
3. Orel Hershiser
4. CC Sabathia
5. Eric Gagne
6. Jake Arrieta
7. Gaylord Perry
8. Randy Jones
9. Dove

10. Warren Spahn
11. Kid Nichols
12. Ted Lyons
13. Charlie Robertson
14. Jamie Moyer at 49 years old
15. Dallas Keuchel
16. ERA
17. Don Newcombe
18. Sandy Koufax
19. "Steve Blass disease"
20. David Clyde

Round 9 - Drafts
1. 1965
2. Rick Monday
3. 3 draft picks
4. Alex Rodriguez
5. Montreal Expos
6. Brian Anderson
7. Gene Lamont
8. Tom Helton
9. D) 15th
10. Adrian Gonzalez
11. Ollie Brown
12. Buster Posey
13. The 42nd round
14. Jeff Clement
15. Matt Cassel
16. Josh Hamilton
17. Detroit Tigers
18. Hillsborough High School
19. 2020
20. Round 20

Round 10 - Contracts
1. No
2. Babe Ruth
3. A) $200/month
4. Dave Winfield
5. Nolan Ryan
6. Albert Belle
7. Pete Rose
8. 3 years, $27,000
9. Eddie Gadedel
10. Adrian Beltre
11. The Commissioner
12. Rube Waddell
13. Bryce Harper
14. Kevin Brow
15. Kevin Brow
16. 2035
17. Curt Schilling
18. George Brett
19. Bulldozer
20. Orange Jell-O

Round 11 - Postseason
1. 1903
2. 1995
3. 11, every single year
4. 2017
5. Vince Coleman
6. Tampa Bay Rays
7. Norm Cash, Willie Mays, Don McMahon, and Stan Williams
8. Atlanta Braves
9. St. Louis Cardinals
10. Curt Schilling in 2001

11. 20 times
12. 3
13. Kyle Schwarber
14. Pitcher
15. Derek Jeter
16. B) 1
17. 1991
18. 1981
19. Boston Red Sox
20. An Earthquake

Round 12 - Tom Brady

1. Boston Red Sox, New York Yankees, Boston Braves
2. Curse of the Bambino
3. George Herman Ruth Jr.
4. True
5. Teased as "Dunn's baby" after he was legally adopted by minor league Baltimore Orioles' manager Jack Dunn. Shortened to "Baby" then "Babe."
6. Swat
7. 714 homeruns
8. Hank Aaron
9. Left-handed Pitcher
10. He threw sidearm
11. February 7, 1894. Bonus: February 6, 1895.
12. One daughter
13. Speeding/Reckless Driving
14. Lou Gehrig
15. 3 World Series
16. 4 World Series
17. Jackie Mitchell
18. Baby Ruth
19. "The House that Ruth Built"
20. The single-season homerun record (29, 54, and 59)

Round 13 - Jackie Robinson

1. Breaking the Color Line/Barrier
2. Brooklyn Dodgers
3. "42"
4. Tennis, junior boys singles
5. Ted Williams (Boston) and Bob Lemon (Indians)
6. Theodore (Teddy) Roosevelt
7. Army
8. Canada with the Montreal Royals
9. Larry Doby
10. 6 seasons
11. 1955
12. Chock Full O' Nuts, an American coffee company
13. Vice President
14. 1962
15. Dr. Martin Luther King Jr.
16. The home Jackie lived in when he played for the Dodgers
17. Analyst
18. Congressional Gold Medal
19. Every team. The MLB retired his number
20. April 15

Round 14 - Controversies

1. Corked Bat
2. Pine Tar Incident
3. Stuffed the ballot box
4. Dick Higham
5. 1994 MLB Strike
6. 4 players
7. Bowie Kuhn
8. Pete Rose
9. Cocaine

10. Barry Bonds, Kevin Brown, Roger Clemens, Lenny Dykstra, Eric Gagne, Jason Giambi, Mark McGwire, Andy Pettitte, Gary Sheffield, Miguel Tejada and many more.
11. 1919
12. Shoeless Joe Jackson
13. PED – Performance Enhancing Drugs
14. Garbage can
15. MLB Owners Collusion from 1985-1987
16. Steve Bartman
17. New York Giants
18. St. Louis Cardinals
19. Wife and children
20. $0.10 Beer Night

Round 15 – AAGPBL
1. All-American Girls Professional Baseball League
2. 12 years, during WWII and shortly after, from 1943-1954
3. Baseball players joined the military, so there were not men to play the sport.
4. Mr. Philip K. Wrigley, yes, like Wrigley Field.
5. 15 teams
6. The US Midwest
7. Do or die!
8. Racine Belles
9. Rockford Peaches
10. Skirts – ouch!
11. Strawberries
12. Overhand – it was baseball after all
13. The Rockford Peaches
14. A League of Their Own
15. Tom Hanks
16. B) $45-$85

17. True
18. Long. They couldn't have short hair.
19. Cuba in Havana
20. 9 players

Round 16 – All-Star Game
1.   1933
2.   Chicago at Comiskey Park
3.   No. The rule was changed in 2017 to whichever of the two teams had the better regular season record
4.   Craig Biggio
5.   Hank Aaron at 21 games
6.   Babe Ruth
7.   Dan Uggla
8.   Aaron Judge
9.   Willie Mays
10. Scott Kazmir
11. 7 How many were starters? 4, first, second, third, and shortstop
12. J.R. Richard
13. Robinson
14. Juan Marichal
15. New York with 9
16. Phil Cavarretta
17. 8 sets
18. Ronald Regan
19. Mike Trout
20. Stan Musial

Round 17 – College Baseball/College World Series
1. Omaha, Nebraska
2. 8 teams
3. Metal
4. Pete Incaviglia

5. Arizona State

6. Rickie Weeks

7. Oregon State Beavers

8. University of Oregon Ducks

9. Pitcher

10. Johnny Bench Award

11. 10 runs

12. 3 games

13. Robin Ventura

14. University of Southern California Trojans

15. George H.W. Bush

16. University of Texas Longhorns

17. 2021: Mississippi State, 2019: Vanderbilt University 2018: Oregon State

18. Florida State University

19. SEC

20. Rod Dedeaux

Round 18 - Hank Aaron

1. Henry

2. Hammer, Hammerin' Hank, Dirty Henry (choose one or all)

3. 1974

4. Willie Mays

5. 7 seasons

6. Milwaukee Braves, Atlanta Braves, Milwaukee Brewers

7. 23 years

8. 3 records: RBI, total bases, and extra base hits

9. 2,297 RBIs

10. 1982

11. "I Had a Hammer"

12. Muhammad Ali

13. True

14. 3 Gold Glove Awards
15. SunTrust Park, Atlanta Braves
16. The Presidential Medal of Freedom
17. Chasing the Dream Foundation
18. National League Batting Award
19. Bobby Thomson
20. Working on an ice truck cutting chunks of ice then carrying it to the customers.

Round 19 – International Baseball

1. 2 teams: Montreal Expos & Toronto Blue Jays
2. Hideo Nomo
3. Canada
4. Cuba
5. Dominican Republic
6. Curacao
7. 20 countries or territories
8. Tokyo
9. An interpreter
10. D) Over 100 countries
11. Japan
12. England
13. Cricket
14. 1992
15. 1982
16. Ichiro Suzuki
17. Slap hitting
18. November – February
19. 19 players
20. World Baseball Classic

Round 20 - AL & NL MVPs

Year	Name	Team	Position
2011	Justin Verlander	Detroit Tigers	SP
2012	Miguel Cabrera	Detroit Tigers	3B
2013	Miguel Cabrera	Detroit Tigers	3B
2014	Mike Trout	LA Angles	CF
2015	Josh Donaldson	Toronto Blue Jays	3B
2016	Mike Trout	LA Angles	CF
2017	Jose Altuve	Houston Astros	2B
2018	Mookie Betts	Boston Red Sox	OF
2019	Mike Trout	LA Angles	CF
2020	Jose Abreu	Chicago White Sox	1B

Year	Name	Team	Position
2011	Ryan Braun	Milwaukee Brewers	OF
2012	Buster Posey	San Francisco Giants	C
2013	Andrew McCutchen	Pittsburg Pirates	OF
2014	Clayton Kershaw	LA Dodgers	SP
2015	Bryce Harper	Washington Nationals	RF
2016	Kris Bryant	Chicago Cubs	3B
2017	Giancarlo Stanton	Miami Marlins	RF
2018	Christian Yelich	Milwaukee Brewers	OF
2019	Cody Bellinger	LA Dodgers	RF
2020	Freddie Freeman	Atlanta Braves	1B

Round 21 - Baseball is a Family Sport

1. D) 432 sets of brothers
2. True
3. 10 sets of twins
4. Hank and Tommie Aaron
5. Bengie, Jose, and Yadier
6. Moses Fleetwood and Weldy Wilberforce Walker
7. Ken Griffey and Ken Griffey Jr.
8. Larkin and Boone
9. Brian Moran
10. Brooks and Frank Robinson
11. Felipe, Jesus, and Matty Alou
12. Moises Alou
13. Dom and Vince DiMaggio
14. Cecil and Prince Fielder
15. Mike and Greg Maddux
16. Paul and Lloyd Waner
17. Barry and Bobby Bonds
18. Tommy and Homer Thompson
19. Manny Mota
20. 3 generations

Round 22 - American League

1. Baltimore Orioles, Boston Americans, Chicago White Stockings, Cleveland Blues, Detroit Tigers, Milwaukee Brewers, Philadelphia Athletics, and Washington Senators
2. Jimmie Fox
3. 1998
4. Mike Mussina
5. White Sox
6. Jack Chesbro
7. Roberto Alomar
8. Rod Carew

9. Boston Red Sox
10. New York Yankees
11. Losing seasons
12. 46 games
13. Indians to the Guardians
14. Detroit Tigers
15. Philadelphia Athletics
16. Ty Cobb
17. Ichiro Suzuki
18. St Louis
19. Tampa Bay Devil Rays
20. Detroit, Chicago, Boston, and Cleveland

Round 23 - National League

1. Boston Beaneaters, Brooklyn Superbas, Chicago Orphans, Cincinnati Reds, New York Giants, Philadelphia Phillies, Pittsburgh Pirates, and St. Louis Perfectos
2. 1876
3. The whole league at its peak!
4. St. Louis Cardinals
5. 1888
6. Game-fixing
7. Bryce Harper at 23
8. Arizona Diamondbacks
9. New York Mets
10. Chicago Cubs
11. Cincinnati Reds
12. Philadelphia Phillies
13. Brooklyn/LA Dodgers
14. St. Louis Cardinals
15. Braves (Boston Beaneaters, Boston Doves, Boston Rustlers, Boston Braves, Boston Bees, Boston Braves, Milwaukee Braves, Atlanta Braves)

16. Philadelphia Phillies
17. Cincinnati Stars
18. LA Dodgers
19. 347 people due to a hurricane
20. Radio broadcast in 1921

Round 24 - Opening Day
1. Boston Red Caps and Philadelphia Athletics
2. William Howard Taft
3. Jimmy Carter, Donald Trump, Joe Biden
4. Mark Buehrle
5. Los Angeles Dodgers and San Francisco Giants
6. Mexico
7. 6 rookies
8. Houston Astros
9. Madison Bumgarner
10. Macklemore
11. Al Woods
12. Bob Feller
13. Tom Seaver
14. New York Mets
15. 1912
16. Chicago White Sox
17. 16 innings
18. 3 games were delayed: 1972, 1990, and 1995
19. Yogi Berra
20. Adam Dunn

Round 25 - AL Stadiums

Team	Stadium	Capacity	Year Built
Los Angeles Angels	Angel Stadium	45,517	1966
Detroit Tigers	Comerica Park	41,083	2000
Boston Red Sox	Fenway Park	37,755	1912
Texas Rangers	Globe Life Field	40,300	1989
Chicago White Sox	Guaranteed Rate Field	40,615	1991
Kansas City Royals	Kauffman Stadium	37,903	1973
Houston Astros	Minute Maid Park	41,168	2000
Baltimore Orioles	Orioles Park at Camden Yards	45,971	1992
Cleveland Indians	Progressive Field	34,788	1994
Oakland Athletics	RingCentral Coliseum	46,847	1966
Toronto Blue Jays	Rogers Centre	49,282	1989
Seattle Mariners	T-Mobile Park	47,929	1999
Minnesota Twins	Target Field	38,544	2010
Tampa Bay Rays	Tropicana Field	25,000	1990
New York Yankees	Yankee Stadium	47,309	2009

Round 26 - NL Stadiums

Team	Stadium	Capacity	Year Built
St. Louis Cardinals	Busch Stadium	45,494	2006
Arizona Diamondbacks	Chase Field	48,686	1998
New York Mets	Citi Field	41,922	2009
Philadelphia Phillies	Citizens Bank Park	42,792	2004
Colorado Rockies	Coors Field	50,445	1995
Los Angeles Dodgers	Dodger Stadium	56,000	1962
Cincinnati Reds	Great American Ball Park	42,319	2003
Miami Marlins	Marlins Park	36,742	2012
Milwaukee Brewers	Miller Park	41,900	2001
Washington Nationals	Nationals Park	41,339	2008
San Francisco Giants	Oracle Park	14,915	2000
San Diego Padres	Petco Park	40,209	2004
Pittsburg Pirates	PNC Park	38,747	2001
Atlanta Braves	SunTrust Park	41,084	2017
Chicago Cubs	Wrigley Field	41,649	1914

Round 27 - Famous Jerseys

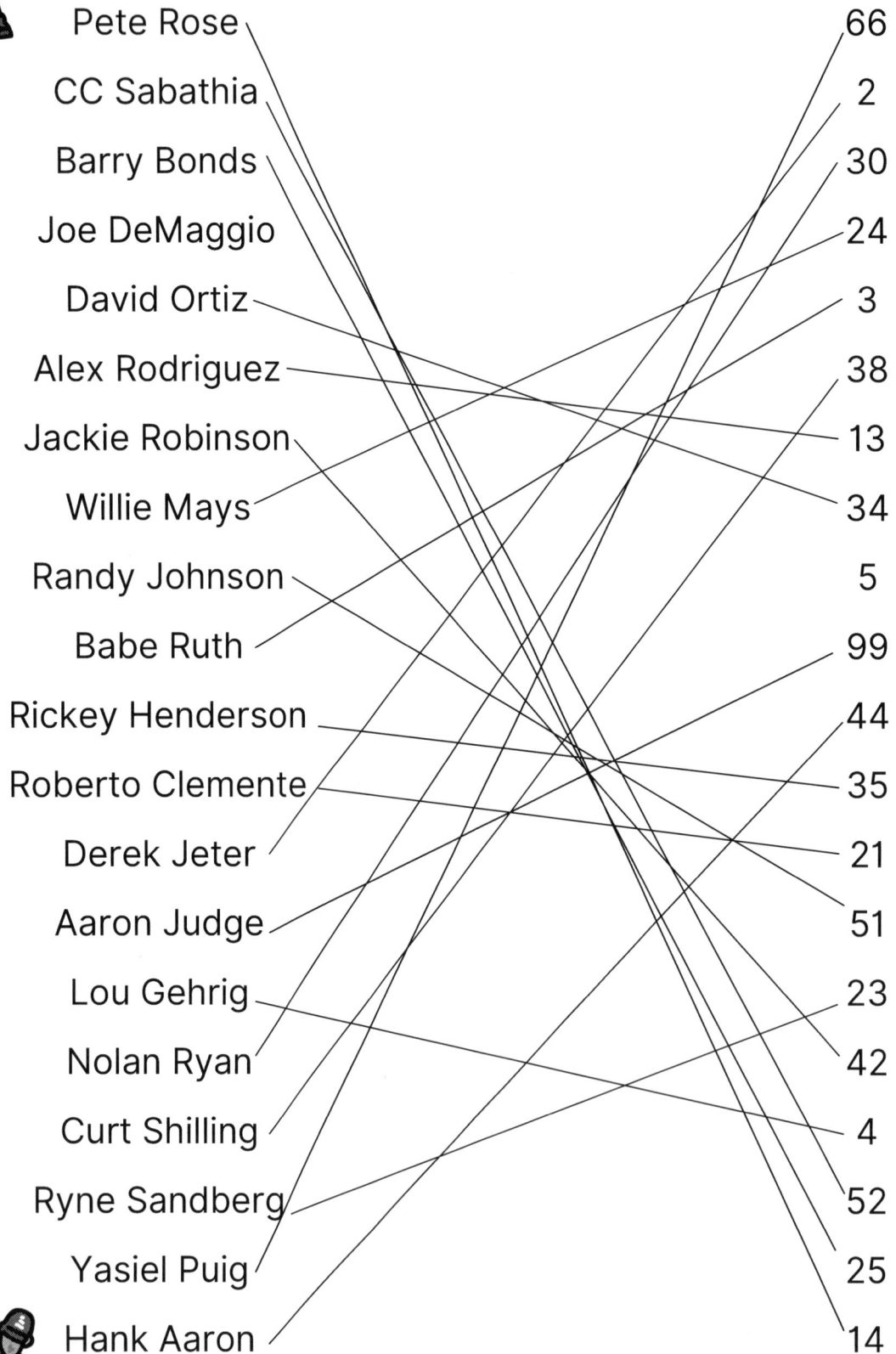

Pete Rose

CC Sabathia

Barry Bonds

Joe DeMaggio

David Ortiz

Alex Rodriguez

Jackie Robinson

Willie Mays

Randy Johnson

Babe Ruth

Rickey Henderson

Roberto Clemente

Derek Jeter

Aaron Judge

Lou Gehrig

Nolan Ryan

Curt Shilling

Ryne Sandberg

Yasiel Puig

Hank Aaron

66

2

30

24

3

38

13

34

5

99

44

35

21

51

23

42

4

52

25

14

ARIZONA DIAMONDBACKS

1. 1998

2. C) 30 players

3. Randy Johnson

4. Bob Brenly

5. Erubiel Durazo

ATLANTA BRAVES

1. Eddie Matthews

2. D) 18 rookies

3. Tony Cloninger

4. 0 losing seasons

5. Larry Wayne Jones Jr.

BALTIMORE ORIOLES

1. Two

2. Raven named "Poe"

3. Pittsburgh Steelers

4. Rod Woodson

5. Jonathan Ogden

BOSTON RED SOX

1. Trading Babe Ruth and repeated loses for decades

2. Ted Williams

3. Brooklyn Robins

4. Jacob Ellsbury

5. Jackie Jensen

CHICAGO CUBS

1. Billy goat
2. Harlem Globetrotters
3. Javier Baez; it means The Magician
4. Harry Caray
5. Ernie Banks

CHICAGO WHITE SOX

1. Michael Jordan
2. Frank Thomas
3. Paul Konerko
4. Sioux City Cornhuskers
5. Chris Sale

CINCINNATI REDS

1. Big Red Machine
2. 15 years old
3. 44 games
4. 4 mascots: Gapper, Mr. Red, Rosie Red, and Mr. Redlegs
5. Johnny Bench

CLEVELAND INDIANS

1. Rapids Rustlers
2. Mistake by the Lake
3. 22 games
4. Major League
5. 455

COLORADO ROCKIES

1. The "mile high" seats exactly 5,280 (1 mile) above sea level
2. Fielding percentage
3. B) 1.4 million bricks
4. Jose Jimenez
5. 2007

DETROIT TIGERS

1. Guitar Hero
2. Al Kaline
3. G-Men
4. Table leg from the clubhouse
5. John Hiller

HOUSTON ASTROS

1. Houston Colts .45
2. They were rainbow
3. Dickie Thon
4. Craig Biggio, Lance Berkman, Jeff Bagwell, and Carlos Beltran
5. Justin Verlander

KANSAS CITY ROYALS

1. American Royal
2. 106 games
3. Whitey Herzog
4. Jorge Soler
5. George Brett

LOS ANGELES ANGELS
1. Katie
2. Mike Trout
3. Jim Abbott
4. Gene Autry
5. Bobby Knoop

LOS ANGELES DODGERS
1. Vin Scully
2. Clayton Kershaw
3. Trolleys
4. Anita Martini
5. Manny Ramirez

MIAMI MARLINS
1. 0 pitchers had winning records
2. Jeremy Hermida
3. Clemente Nunez
4. Rene Lachemann
5. 2012

MILWAUKEE BREWER
1. Seattle Pilots
2. C) 8 hours 6 minutes
3. Bob Uecker
4. Rollie Fingers
5. Robin Yount

MINNESOTA TWINS

1. The Twin Cities
2. Cesar Tovar
3. LA Lakers and San Francisco Warriors
4. 1961
5. 2019

NEW YORK METS

1. 2012
2. Tim Tebow
3. Metropolitans
4. Garth Brooks
5. Tom Seaver

NEW YORK YANKEES

1. Thurman Munson
2. Derek Jeter
3. Hideki Matsui
4. Murderers Row
5. Baltimore Orioles (not related to the modern-day Orioles)

OAKLAND ATHLETICS

1. 36 Games
2. Reggie Jackson
3. 20 bases, successful 12 times
4. 7 times, all of them.
5. Catfish Hunter

Round 33 - Team by Team VI

PHILADELPHIA PHILLIES

1. Chase Utley

2. B) 23 games

3. Blue Jays

4. 1964

5. Billy Hamilton

PITTSBURGH PIRATES

1. "We are Family"

2. The Flying Dutchman

3. Roberto Clemente

4. Josh Harrison

5. They "pirated" players from the collapsing Players' League

SAN DIEGO PADRES

1. Nate Colbert

2. Ray Kroc

3. 6 seasons

4. Tony Gwynn

5. C. Arnholt Smith

SAN FRANCISCO GIANTS

1. 1962

2. Barry Bonds

3. Madison Bumgarner

4. 269.1 innings (269 works, too)

5. Mel Ott

SEATTLE MARINERS

1. 15 seasons
2. 6 pitchers
3. Lenny Randle
4. 3 teams
5. 42 pitchers

ST LOUIS CARDINALS

1. August Busch Jr.
2. Rogers Hornsby
3. Enos Slaughter
4. Albert Pujols
5. D) $147 million

TAMPA BAY RAYS

1. Devil Rays
2. Stephen King
3. Alex Colome
4. Kevin Kiermaier
5. Geremi Gonzalez

TEXAS RANGERS

1. Eddie Stanky
2. Mike Hargrove
3. Rusty Greer
4. Ivan Rodriguez
5. Gaylord Perry

Round 35- Team by Team VIII

TORONTO BLUE JAYS

1. (Labatt Brewing Company)

2. Dead Fish

3. Roy Halladay

4. BJ Birdy

5. Kevin Pillar

WASHINGTON NATIONALS

1. Montreal Expos

2. D) 25 runs

3. "Natinals"

4. Jordan Zimmerman

5. 3 players: A.J. Cole, Derek Norris, and Brad Peacock

Made in the USA
Columbia, SC
27 March 2022